vocal duet and string quartet
(score and parts *plus* piano/vocal)

T0055828

jason robert brown in this room

contents

ISBN 978-1-4584-0025-3

HAL•LEONARD®
CORPORATION
7777 W. BLUEMOUND RD. P.O. BOX 13819 MILWAUKEE, WI 53213

In Australia Contact:
Hal Leonard Australia Pty. Ltd.
4 Lentara Court
Cheltenham, Victoria, 3192 Australia
Email: ausadmin@halleonard.com

Visit Hal Leonard Online at
www.halleonard.com

about the song

JASON ROBERT BROWN composed "In This Room" for his wedding, where it was performed by singers Lauren Kennedy and Rozz Morehead and the string quartet Ethel. "In This Room" was recorded by Lauren Kennedy with Rozz Morehead on the album *Here and Now*, which is available on PS Classics. Jason Robert Brown's full-length album collaboration with Lauren Kennedy, *Songs of Jason Robert Brown*, is also available on PS Classics.

This edition of "In This Room" includes the full score of the original vocal duet and string quartet version, a set of string parts, and the piano/vocal duet version of the song. Changes have been applied to the piano part of the piano/vocal duet version to make for a more idiomatic work. The piano part in the full score version is a reduction of all string parts.

jason
robert
brown

IN THIS ROOM

recorded by Lauren Kennedy with Rozz Morehead on the CD *Here and Now*

Music and Lyrics by
JASON ROBERT BROWN

2

wait, he said,— 'til I feel the tip—— of—— your fing - er in—— my hand.—— I will

come, she said,— when you move to me.— when you step a - way—— from the o - pen door— I will

wait, they said.— I will come, they said,— while the wa - ter turned— to sand.— Wait - ing...

9

love,_____ clear - ing ground, cut - ting paths through the clay.____ There is

love____ in this room,____ stand - ing meek - ly be - hind you,____ keep - ing

all things that blind you a - way.

Some-one send me o - ver the cliff— and o -

Some-one send me o - ver the cliff— and o -

IN THIS ROOM

recorded by Lauren Kennedy with Rozz Morehead on the CD *Here and Now*

VIOLIN I

Music and Lyrics by
JASON ROBERT BROWN

IN THIS ROOM

VIOLIN II

recorded by Lauren Kennedy with Rozz Morehead on the CD *Here and Now*

Music and Lyrics by
JASON ROBERT BROWN